# Confronting Today's Prophecies

Leroy Vincent

Published by RWG Publishing, 2022.

While every precaution has been taken in the preparation of this book, the publisher assumes no responsibility for errors or omissions, or for damages resulting from the use of the information contained herein.

CONFRONTING TODAY'S PROPHECIES

**First edition. February 21, 2022.**

Copyright © 2022 Leroy Vincent.

Written by Leroy Vincent.

## Also by Leroy Vincent

How to Avoid Self-Deception!
You Will Be Given Power: The Holy Spirit Comes Upon You
What Is the Best Way to Begin a New Season?
A Historical Watershed Moment
Allow the Box to Go: God Cannot Fit in a Box
Confronting Today's Prophecies

# Table of Contents

Confronting Today's Prophecies ............................................................. 1
What does the Bible have to say about the Most Important Thing? 3
The Most Powerful in the Kingdom ........................................................ 5
The Most Important Commandment ...................................................... 7
What is the Purpose of Prophecy? ........................................................... 9
Which one is the most difficult to complete? ...................................... 11

# Confronting Today's Prophecies

"What is the Lord saying for this year?" I am asked every year. For years, I had been searching and asking the Lord what He had planned for His people for the coming year. Because of my upbringing and environment, I found myself always including more of an "army" and "militant" attitude when delivering the Lord's word. You must realize that whenever you get a prophecy from the Lord, it will be delivered through an imperfect vessel. So, when we hear the Lord's voice, it must come through our experiences, thoughts, attitudes, theology, and doctrines. Can you imagine the prophetic message having to pass through all of that before it comes out of our mouths to deliver to the person to whom we are prophesying? This is why it is critical that we shrink in order for Christ to increase in us. It's critical that we don't put our concepts, beliefs, or traditions on a pedestal. To put it another way, when the Lord speaks to us, we should never let our faith stand in the way of conveying the message He has for His people.

# What does the Bible have to say about the Most Important Thing?

After much prayer and examining the scriptures, I've come to the conclusion that the prophetic is a means that God has chosen to convey His love to humanity and teach them what grace and mercy actually are. What I've just heard from a few prophetic folks is diametrically opposed to Christ's message and the New Testament. Please understand that I admire and appreciate these individuals. Many of them are friends whom I adore, but we must always prioritize Jesus before flesh. As many of you know, I never confront people and do my best to avoid being unpleasant to them. I am a staunch believer in just spreading God's love and grace to everyone because I feel that the love we have for one another will reveal who are His (Christ's) disciples. While reading a few of the words for the year written by a few, but not all, of the members on this council, I found myself pained in spirit as I read about how we are an army...army...and army. And the "word" appeared to be the same one that this woman uses every year on "God is building up an army." Let us now turn to the Bible to see what the Lord has to say regarding the word "army" in the New Testament.

The term "army" appears only four times in the New Testament. Three times it refers to Old Testament scripture, and the fourth time it mentions the army of the white horse rider in The Book of Revelation. Now, we can find the word "love" over 400 times in the New Testament! Yes, four hundred times! Do I believe we're a military force? Absolutely! But we must also consider our Model, our genuine Mentor, our Leader, Savior, and Lord. Jesus is that ideal person!

# The Most Powerful in the Kingdom

Hearing prophetic words from some of these people seems to instill in us a sense of rage toward sinners, our country, our leaders, and those who do not see things our way and do not share our convictions. Please understand that I love these individuals and recognize that they are doing and saying what they have been taught for the majority of their life, but that does not make it acceptable when dealing with people who believe you are "the voice" of the Lord. Let me ask you a question: in the kingdom of God, is it better to be a fighting army or to be a servant? Let's take a peek at the Bible's New Testament.

1. The disciples approached Jesus at that time and questioned, "Who is the greatest in the kingdom of heaven?"

2. He summoned a small child and asked him to stand among them.

3. And Jesus added: "You will never enter the kingdom of heaven unless you change and become like tiny children, I tell you the truth.

4. As a result, in the kingdom of heaven, whoever humbles himself like this kid is the greatest.

Do we see a fighter or a lover in Jesus when we examine his life? Do we see someone who slammed the president and other officials, inciting the people to believe that God is about to judge this country, or do we see Jesus who RESPECTED the terrible ruler of the day, saying, "Give to Caesar what belongs to Caesar," and never once bashing those in power.....ever! The RELIGIOUS SYSTEM was the only one with whom Jesus had a problem. At all of His teachings, Jesus emphasized dealing with one's own sin, plucking the plank out of one's own eye, judgment beginning in the Lord's home (you), judging not of others, and so on.

In other words, Jesus never focused on chastising sinners, opposing Him, or any of the other things that some of these prophets are stirring up. "A smooth answer drives away wrath," the Bible states. "Stoke up controversy by making people angry so you'll think you're being persecuted for the cause of the Gospel," it doesn't state.

# The Most Important Commandment

Luke 22:34-40 The Pharisees gathered after hearing that Jesus had silenced the Sadducees. "Teacher, which is the greatest commandment in the Law?" one of them, a legal expert, put him to the test. "Love the Lord your God with all your heart, all your soul, and all your mind," Jesus said. The first and most important commandment is to love your neighbor as yourself. "Love your neighbor as you love yourself," says the second. These two commandments are the foundation of the entire Law and Prophets."

So, what were the prophets looking forward to when they arrived to planet Earth? Love, love, love, love, love, love, love, love, love, love

Coming to earth as God's magnificent Son would revolutionize the way we live, treat people, and PROPHESY! We are expected to respect people in positions of power (according to the New Testament). We are commanded to love those who hate us. "Love your enemies and pray for those who persecute you," we are told. 5:44 in Matthew

"Thou preparest a table before me in the midst of my enemies: thou anointest my head with oil; my cup overfloweth," Psalms says.

When we think of Jesus, we should remember that He overturned tables IN THE TEMPLE OF GOD, not in the White House, not in the local town because a new law had been made that He did not agree with......no, He overturned tables in the temple. What is the significance of the temple?

3:16 in 1 Corinthians "Are you unaware that you are a temple of God and that the Holy Spirit resides within you?" He concentrated on the within rather than the exterior once more. Why are some of these prophets so focused on the outside world? Because it seems better to point the finger at others rather than examine ourselves.

# What is the Purpose of Prophecy?

We must first establish in our thoughts that we follow God's entire council, but that as prophets, we walk under a NEW COVENANT AND ONLY A NEW COVENANT. There is a significant distinction between Old Testament and New Testament prophets. Only "edification, exhortation, and comfort" are the principles for New Testament prophecy. NEW TESTAMENT PROPHETS CAN AND WILL MOVE INTO THE ARENA OF INSTRUCTION, REBUKE, AND DIRECTION, BUT IT MUST FIRST PASS THROUGH JESUS' BLOOD AND GRACE BEFORE IT CAN BE DELIVERED TO THE PEOPLE.

Even while some of these prophets (not all of them) are declaring God's vengeance on our nation, government, people, laws, and so on, it is not in agreement with any of Jesus' words. Jesus is our role model! He is the DIRECTION TO THE FATHER. That is to say, in order to reach the Father, we must be like ME (Jesus) or go through Me (Jesus). As a result, we must go to the Father THROUGH THE SON. Have you grasped what I've just said? PASS THROUGH the Son. What does it mean to say "through Him"? It translates to "say as I talk," "walk as I walk," "love as I love," and "be as I am in the land."

"Herein is our love perfected," 1 John 4:17 says, "that we may have boldness in the day of judgment: for as he is, so are we in this world."

What? Is THIS EXACTLY HOW I AM TO BE, WALK, AND TALK, AS HE WAS ON THE EARTH? Yes! He loved the sinners and invited them to eat with Him, He loved the tax collector (which was considered bad in those days), and He simply told a woman CAUGHT

IN THE MIDDLE OF ADULTERY AND DRAGGED INTO THE STREET, WHO HAD NO TIME TO FEEL BAD OR REPENT OF HER SIN, "I AM NOT YOUR ACCUSER" and then told her, "Go and sin no more." WOW! Why do we still have prophets today that prophecy from a vengeful spirit? Why are today's prophets behaving like John the Baptist? Why do some prophets predict that "birds falling from the sky" will be a symbol of God's wrath? Why? Because they are unfamiliar with the Jesus of the Bible, who loved, forgave, and welcomed them into His presence.

The Holy Scriptures remind us in 1 John 4:16-18, "And we have known and believed in God's love for us. God is love, and whoever lives in love lives in God, and God lives in him. Herein is our love perfected, so that we may have boldness in the day of judgment: for we are in this world as he is. Dread has no place in love, but pure love casts it out, because fear torments. Fearful people are not made perfect in love."

Keep this in mind.

# Which one is the most difficult to complete?

1. Deny ourselves, discipline our body, remove the log out of our own eye, fearfully and tremblingly work out our own redemption.
OR
2. Judge others, threaten individuals with God's vengeance, concentrate on removing the powers that rule us in our country, and exhort those who are in sin to repent before God or face the consequences?

The first statement is the answer. Why? Because we all know how difficult it is to look in the mirror and fight with ourselves to walk with integrity and greatness, to remove the plank from our own eye that prevents us from loving those who have injured us, and so on.

"It is God's lovingkindness that draws men to repentance," the New Testament declares. This phrase sums it all up......love.

Whatever you do or say, if it is not done or said from a place of deep, passionate love for people, it is and will always be merely a clanging sign that is ineffective. Let's not add fuel to the fire of those who despise God. Let us not encourage those who do not come in the name of "FOR GOD SO LOVED THE WORLD..."

In 1 John 4:7-8, the New Testament says: "Let us, beloved, love one another, for love is from God, and anyone loves is born of God and knows God. He who does not love does not know God, for God is love."

We cannot know God unless we love others. A person who does not love people, but rather criticizes and judges them, is not a child of God.

Assist me in launching the greatest revolution the world has ever seen. That is God's love for people.

# Don't miss out!

Visit the website below and you can sign up to receive emails whenever Leroy Vincent publishes a new book. There's no charge and no obligation.

https://books2read.com/r/B-A-TQWI-ZZXVB

BOOKS2READ

Connecting independent readers to independent writers.

# Also by Leroy Vincent

How to Avoid Self-Deception!
You Will Be Given Power: The Holy Spirit Comes Upon You
What Is the Best Way to Begin a New Season?
A Historical Watershed Moment
Allow the Box to Go: God Cannot Fit in a Box
Confronting Today's Prophecies

# About the Publisher

Accepting manuscripts in the most categories. We love to help people get their words available to the world.

Revival Waves of Glory focus is to provide more options to be published. We do traditional paperbacks, hardcovers, audio books and ebooks all over the world. A traditional royalty-based publisher that offers self-publishing options, Revival Waves provides a very author friendly and transparent publishing process, with President Bill Vincent involved in the full process of your book. Send us your manuscript and we will contact you as soon as possible.

Contact: Bill Vincent at rwgpublishing@yahoo.com www.rwgpublishing.com

www.ingramcontent.com/pod-product-compliance
Lightning Source LLC
Chambersburg PA
CBHW031220081025
33728CB00087B/2152